Secrets Of The Internet Millionaire Mind

$S + C + E = \$$

you rock.
Matt

www.$$$$$-$.com

by Matt Bacak

New York

D0111877

Secrets of the Internet Millionaire Mind

by Matt Bacak

ISBN: 1-60037-052-7 (Paperback)

Published by:

MORGAN · JAMES
THE ENTREPRENEURIAL PUBLISHER ™
www.morganjamespublishing.com

Morgan James Publishing, LLC

1225 Franklin Ave. Ste 325

Garden City, NY 11530-1693

Toll Free 800-485-4943

www.MorganJamesPublishing.com

Habitat
for Humanity®
Peninsula
Building Partner

Interior Design & Layout by:
Bonnie Bushman
bbushman@bresnan.net

Acknowledgements

I want to thank all those who helped me become the person that could write this book. Those who shaped my "Internet Millionaire Mind" were not always the kind, loving teachers that we usually thank. In this journey, my hardships were some of my greatest teachers. I want to share my sincere appreciation for the dedication, hard-work and creativity of my second family at my offices, my staff. I owe so much success and nights that I actually did sleep to my team - thank you!

Table of Contents

Foreword

When it comes to success as an Internet entrepreneur one thing matters more than anything else.

Without this one thing success will likely elude you.

Here's a story that illustrates what I mean...

A couple years ago two entrepreneurs each started their own Internet business.

These two entrepreneurs were very similar. Both were average students in school. Both were smart and likable. And both were filled with ambitious dreams for the future.

Well, recently these two Internet entrepreneurs met a seminar.

They were both still very much alike. Both were happily married. Both had children. And both, as it turned out, had started their Internet businesses marketing very similar products to the same type of prospects. And they were both still involved with their businesses.

But there was a difference. A big difference.

You see, one of them was attending the seminar hoping to finally figure out the elusive secret they had been missing. Because they were still struggling to have any real success with their Internet business.

The other entrepreneur had become an Internet millionaire and was invited to be one of the speakers at that seminar where they both met.

So, "what made the difference?", you might ask.

Because it isn't always a matter of intelligence, talent, or dedication. It's not like one of them wanted success and the other one didn't.

Foreword

The difference was that one of them had taken the time to develop their Internet Millionaire Mind. The other had not.

Can guess which one was the Internet millionaire?

Yes. The millionaire was the one who had this most important of success factors working for them. While the other entrepreneur was still struggling to "put all the pieces together."

They were trying to do business without the thinking necessary to create massive success for yourself. The thinking you get when you develop your Internet Millionaire Mind.

When it comes to developing your own Internet Millionaire Mind there is no one I would recommend more highly than my great friend Matt Bacak.

Secrets of the Internet Millionaire Mind

I've watched first-hand as Matt started his Internet business from scratch and went on to become an Internet millionaire.

Best of all, he's mastered the art of helping others develop the mindset necessary to duplicate his incredible success.

So, you've made a very wise decision by getting this book into your hands. It's definitely the right step toward developing your own Internet Millionaire Mind.

Now, get ready for all the benefits, freedom, and success that comes with it as you dive into this priceless resource!

— Jason Oman

Introduction

I am sharing information in this book that I have never shared with the public.

Therefore, I want to make sure that you understand just how important this information really is. I mean, there are tips, techniques and methods written here that have never been revealed to the public. I have only shared this powerful information behind closed doors.

In this book, we are going to cover the nine common characteristics of Internet-Millionaires, which you need to know. We are going to discuss some case studies of "traditional" Internet Millionaires and I am going to give you some case studies of a few Internet Millionaire "accidents." Did you know there are people who are just accidental Internet Millionaires? They make millions of dollars online, and I am going to share with you who they are and what it was that made their Internet Millionaire "accident" happen for them.

Folks, I just want to let you know, being an Internet Millionaire is amazing. The best thing in the world is having money to spend and never having to worry about bills. There are no more worries about how much money you have. There are no more worries about what you can order when you're sitting down at a restaurant. There are no worries about paying a valet a few extra bucks to park your car. That's what we're talking about. How can you get into that situation? How can you change your life so that you can have all the things that you've ever wanted? I'm talking about super-sizing your lifestyle, so that there are no more worries about petty expenses.

It's about learning how to choose where you work. For example, I have a friend who's decided that he wants to work in the middle of his pool with his laptop. And he can do that if he chooses, because, that's what being an Internet Millionaire allows you to do. You can work at the beach; you can work at home, or in the middle of your pool! My friend, Mike Stewart, and I often go out on his boat, we make money sitting there enjoying ourselves on the lake. I mean, how cool is that? Just imagine sailing, having fun, and making money.

Or even my own personal goal, I want to be flying my plane making money. I am already fulfilling a lifetime dream by becoming a pilot. Just imagine all those dreams that you have for yourself. I encourage you to write at least five goals down that may seem impossible in your current life. The information I am sharing with you in this book, will allow you to make your personal dreams come true. I am giving you specific Action Steps. I am giving you some amazing secrets.

Just imagine setting your own work hours, having the family time you crave, never having to rely on an

after school program, home schooling your children if you choose, and traveling the world. My family has been all over the world. We can do that because of the power of the information that I am sharing with you in this book.

How would you like to buy any car you want? Not long ago my car broke down; I had driven the car since my senior year in high school. I was determined to drive it until it fell apart, and then go out, and buy myself any car I wanted. It finally broke down beyond reasonable repair and I was able to pay cash for a sporty Mercedes hardtop convertible. Even better, by using the powerful information that I'm about to share with you, the next day I was able to send an email that allowed me to make back the money that I paid for my car.

What you should see that this is the ticket to controlling your own destiny and to living the lifestyle you choose. You might be sitting there thinking, "Matt, who are you to tell me how to develop the Internet Millionaire Mind?" Remember, it was not always hunky dory for me. I drove the same car so long for two reasons: The first was my determination to become a millionaire; the second was that for a portion of the time I was broke.

My first apartment after college was in Snellville, Georgia. It was a small one-bedroom apartment about the size of my office here at the company. I sat on a small couch and slept on a cot. I did my dishes in the same sink that I washed my hands in every morning after I went to the bathroom. Can you imagine? I do not know if any of you have ever been in that situation, but it was not fun. I went flat broke, bankrupt, in less than three years. Then, I made my first million online, and now my main company is a multimillion-dollar operation.

I have companies that are doing amazing things-making money quicker that I ever thought possible. So,

to answer that question, "Matt, who are you to tell me this information?" I started at the bottom and made it. I have worked behind the scenes to help some of the giants in the industry make it.

A lot of my clients and 'BIG' guys in the industry are teaching you this same information that I originally taught them. So, in addition to the proven success of my teaching, you really should get your education from the horse's mouth. The most important to realize is that I'm no different than you. I have worked hard to get where I am. Moreover, I truly care about you as a person with dreams and goals and I care about your results.

Everyone who has been around me knows that I want to see everybody successful. In fact, I was thinking about my students and how to make them more successful and it hit me. I realized that I can build systems for my students and give them all the information, all the techniques, and all the strategies

Introduction

that I have used in my life and in my business to make millions of dollars for myself. But do you know what? If you don't have it "right" between your ears, NO system works for you. That's why this course has been developed - to create a millionaire mindset.

Chapter 1
Goals

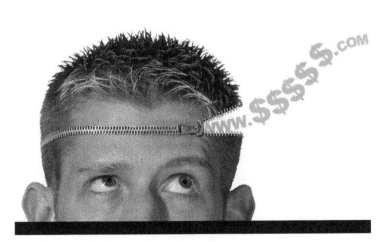

Goals

First, I set goals for myself. I remember my first goal on the internet was to make $100. It wasn't to make a million. My next goal was to make $1,000. Then after that was to make $10,000. When I made my $10,000, I decided my next goal would be to make $ 100,000.

When I made my first $100,000, I didn't do it in a year. No. I didn't do it in a month. I did it in one hour. After that happened so suddenly, I just said, "I figured it out. All I have to do is do this 10 times and bam! I make my goal." And you know what? I made my first million in less than three months after I made my first $100,000 in that hour.

Now the cool thing is that I set new goals. The reason I'm sharing this with you has nothing to do with me. It's about you, because I want you to get your goals straight. So that you know that your first goal is not, "oh, I wanna make $1 million." Because if you haven't made a $1,000 on the internet, how the heck are you going to make your first $100,000 or first million? You have to make $1,000 before you can make your $100,000 dollars. You have to make $100,000 before you can make a million dollars. However, you have to set your goals.

My first new goal is to do $1 million in one day. I already have that day planned; I know when I'm going to do it. After that, my goal is to make $1 million in an hour. Then to make $1 million in a minute. Can it happen? Absolutely, I know it can.

As we cover the nine common characteristics of Internet Millionaires, you see that we all plan out every dollar we expect to make.

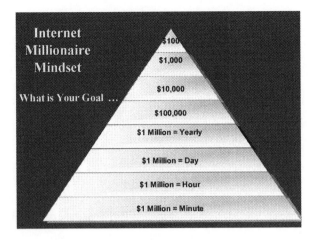

Remember that I said you have to be "Right" between your ears. That's where you have to be in the "right" mindset because your thoughts turn into your language. Your language turns into action, and your action turns into results.

Now, the result we're talking about in this course is Money. So, get your greed glands going because I'm about to tell you how to make it happen. It doesn't matter who you are, what color you are, what you know, or where you grew up. If you develop this mindset, amazing things will happen for you.

Now if you think about this... Your thoughts turn into your language. Your language turns into action and your action turns into results. You may have heard that before and most people say, "Oh yeah, I might know that." BUT here's the deal: there are two different types of language people use. I want you to be aware of this.

Some people have **Indecisive language**.... They are saying things to themselves right now like, "Well, I already know this stuff." Well, maybe you have heard something like this before, but you don't know what I have planned for you later. So here is the kind of words or phrases that indecisive people say: "I'll try to do it." "I may do it." "I might get around to it." Here in the South, we might say, "I'm fixin' to."

That's indecisive language, and that's going to stop people from getting into Action to get the Results they want. What you want to have is **Decisive language**. You want to be thinking and you must say, "I will do this. I must do this." I don't know if you noticed earlier when I said, "I will make that happen." You want to have those types of words coming out of your mouth. Not only coming out of your mouth, but also coming out of your head. You have to have this mindset.

IMPORTANT: When you move to the next part of the equation, when you move into <u>action,</u> there are two important "F" words. The first F word FEAR can stop you from reaching your goals, stop you from super-sizing your lifestyle.

You may have heard this before - probably from Brian Tracy. You hear many speakers saying it...

They say that FEAR is False Evidence Appearing Real.

<u>FEAR</u>
False
Evidence
Appearing
Real

Well, I thought about that and they are right. But here's my spin on it, it's not only False Evidence Appearing Real, but it's also, False EDUCATION Appearing Real.

FEAR
False
Education
Appearing
Real

Some people are educated the wrong way. That is why I want to share this information with you. If you live in FEAR, you will never get the results that you want.

The other "F" word is FAITH. You've gotta have faith. Have faith in yourself. Have faith in you husband. Have faith in your wife. Have faith in your kids. Have faith in your business. Have faith in your idea. You will see results! Have faith in other people, too. Not having faith in other people is a huge problem that many of us have. You have to have faith. Your Faith moves you forward through ACTION and leads you to the RESULT that you desire.

Let me ask you a question. Do you know your personal cost of not developing the Internet Millionaire Mindset? Do you know the actual hard cost? I'll tell you one of the costs for me, was looking in the eyes of my child and my wife at Christmas and knowing that I couldn't give them what I wanted to give them. I couldn't give them what they wanted or needed.

The thing that changed my life, and I do not often share this story. I grew up in a small town outside of Youngstown, Ohio, a hard working steel town called Cortland. We didn't have much money. My parents gave me a budget. My parents told me, "If you want to buy expensive shoes, and the cool clothes that the other kids are wearing. You have to earn the money for yourself. You have to go out there and make it happen."

I said, "Okay, I will." I went out and got a couple of paper routes.

One of the last stops on my paper route was an assisted living community (or as I called it then, an old folks' home). I would sit around and talk to them. The old people would say, "Boy, if I was your age" and "I wish I would've done this" or "I could've done this and I should've done that," .They were telling me all the things and they wished they had accomplished in their lives.

I remember many of them saying to me "If I had the money I would have invested in stocks, or I would have started business because I could have made a lot of money."

I remember one day, I was on my way home from my paper routes. Instead of passing by the waterfall at the old mill, I rode my bike down to the water with my paper-bag on my shoulder. I threw it on my bike; I ran underneath the waterfall and made a promise to myself: "I will never end up like those people – full of regret. I do not want to end up like that. I don't want to ever say, 'I wish I had done this, or I wish I could've done that.'"

I want to live life without regrets. I want to emphasize that to you. Think about all of the things you could have done, you should have done, and you would have done, but you did not. It was **fear** that stopped you from doing those things. I want to challenge you to start moving in **faith**, because absolute miracles will happen for you.

Chapter 2
Millionaire Report and Statistics

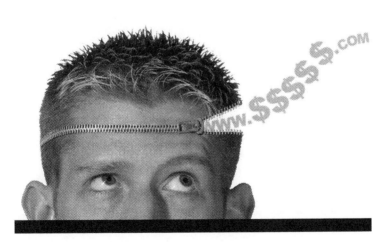

Millionaire Report and Statistics

According to Forbes' 19th annual list of the richest people (published in 2006), there are 793 (US-dollar) billionaires in the world. I'm not talking about millionaires, I'm talking about billionaires. YES, billionaires with a "B".

Back in 1997, Forbes even predicted that there would soon be a new status: Centibillionaire defined as a person to be worth more than $100 billion. Another angle is to look at countries outside the US that have a growing high networth class, per World Wealth Report in 2004, India had 69,800 millionaires. Another 2003 report revealed 1,400 people around the world become millionaires each day. Are you going to be next? You have to decide which day is yours.

Secrets of the Internet Millionaire Mind

Donald Trump went from millionaire to broke, to billionaire. Even Ivana (his ex-wife), loaned him money when he was dead broke, because she knew that he has the Millionaire Mindset. If Donald Trump and his goofy hair can acquire the millionaire mindset, you can.

Chapter 3
Internet Millionaire Accidents

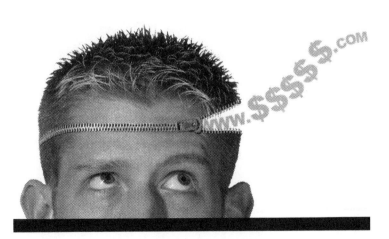

Internet Millionaire Accidents

Now, I want to share with you some Internet Millionaire Accidents. Have you heard of Armand Morin? Armand Morin is called the generator guy. He is a great internet marketer and a good friend of mine. Armand Morin created a toolbar.

This toolbar he created, put together the websites that used and other sites he found useful. He saved them, similar to our saving web sites in the Internet Explorer's *Favorites*. Except he put them into a toolbar. He started selling these toolbars, which were... just his Favorites list... and in less than three months, he made over a $1 million dollars. He did not expect it to happen, it just happened. Accidentally because he was in ACTION.

Have you heard of Morgan Westerman? You have probably seen his *Interviews with God*. *Interviews with God* is a public domain poem.

Note: Public Domain are books and movies, etc. that are so old they no longer have a copyright in force. They can often be found on the internet for use. There are an infinite number of topics & books for the taking. You can actually go to these sites, find materials, and after making certain that the copyrights have expired, you can use them for your own. You can slap on the title <u>Think and Grow Rich</u>. Ever heard of that book? The book is in public domain, you can get a copy of it, take off Napoleon Hill's name, and put your name on it.

So Morgan Westerman took a public domain poem and he turned it into a flash movie. The "movie" showed breathtaking landscapes with inspirational music and then lines of the poem would pop up. This movie was delivered to millions by email, it became viral because people loved it and passed it on. You may have received it several times. In the course of six months, he made a $1 million dollars.

Chapter 3 **Internet Millionaire Accidents**

Morgan and Armand never realized this would happen. There are so many opportunities out there for you to make a lot of money. Think about the stories I have told you; think about the statistics I've given you.

Chapter 4

Nine Common Characteristics of an Internet Millionaire

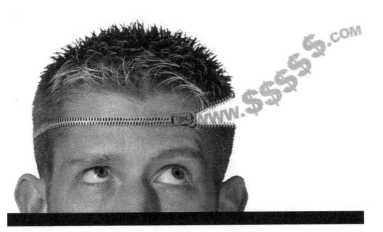

Nine Common Characteristics of an Internet Millionaire

1) Blame versus Learn

2) Take Quick Decisive Action

3) Trust Gut/Trust Intuition

4) Single Focused

5) Marketing Focused

6) Education Focused- Understand Importance of Continuing Education

7) Not Afraid to Make Mistakes- Receive Feedback

8) Model and Swipe

9) Build Team "Success is a Team Sport"

Number One: BLAME VERSUS LEARN

An Internet Millionaire never blames anyone else for his or her failures. Society seems to encourage us to play the blame or victim game but you cannot develop the Mindset you need, if you fall into this trap. Internet Millionaires say, "I just learned a lesson from that." They do not blame. They learn from their mistakes. They learn from other people's mistakes.

Number Two: TAKE QUICK DECISIVE ACTION

The second two common characteristic of Internet Millionaires is decisiveness. They take quick, decisive action. You could say that they are action oriented. When they see an opportunity, they jump on it. They go after their goal wholeheartedly. You have to be decisive. The major cause of failure is lack of ACTION and that often can be traced back to taking months to make decisions. If you are like that, you are never going to get anywhere. The first one to make a decision usually wins.

Mark Joyner, (The Godfather of Internet Marketing), recently came to one of my events. I got to spend some time with him; it was pretty cool, because the student became the teacher. I said, "Mark, what would you say is the number one trait that most Internet Millionaires have?" and he says, "Man, we go first. You know; that we make it happen."

They are action oriented.

Number Three: TRUST GUT/TRUST INTUITION

I am going to tell you right now: Ladies, trust your intuition. Guys, trust your gut. Internet Millionaires trust themselves. You have to trust in yourself, in your gut or in your intuition. You have to have faith in yourself to make your dreams happen.

Any time I break that rule, I regret it. Sometimes you just want to trust someone or that a project will work out when you know in your gut that you should walk away. Trust your gut.

Number Four: SINGLE FOCUSED

Internet Millionaires are single-focused. What I mean is, they have a business and they focus on that one

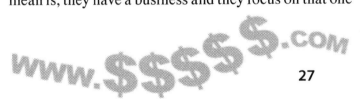

core business, their niche. You see them make things happen quickly because, they focus on single goals. All efforts lead to accomplishing the main goal!

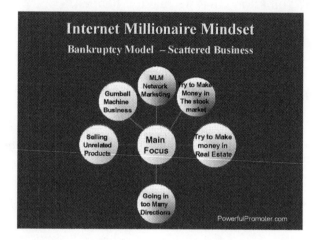

Here is a bankruptcy model; I know this from first hand experience what the basic model looks like. Because I went bankrupt. I lost everything that I had. So please be HONEST WITH YOURSELF ABOUT THIS.

Of course being scattered can look many different ways. For this example, let's say you have a core business.

Then you join a network marketing organization or MLM because you love their (unrelated) product. That is what you are doing until one night it is "Uh, okay, then I'll be a real estate investor." Then come all these real estate seminars. That's when it falls apart. For me, I realized that I was selling 200 unrelated products on the internet (too many targets to aim for).

This is the point too many people reach. They are too diverse, have no idea of what to do to re-organize. They are not sure of where they are or where they're going. That is the Bankruptcy Model. You know, this path will pull you away from your goals; it will pull you away from your vision.

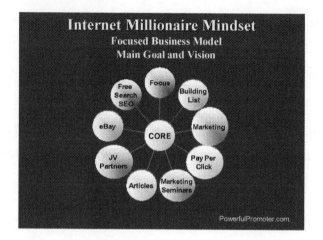

Here is the model you do want. You have to focus. Remember, the fourth characteristic is staying focused on one single core business. Every effort supports the core. Selling your products on eBay – not selling everything you can on eBay. You might add search engine traffic optimizing to your marketing efforts and start focusing on the results. However, remember it is all about the core business. Then you could write articles and get them out on the internet. Next, you might focus on joint ventures and finding people to help get your market out. You must keep the momentum.

You must focus on pay per clicks, on building email lists. Then it happens.

The internet millionaire goes to marketing seminars and always focuses on his business. All of their time and energy stays focused on their goal, the vision for their company, the dream they have for their life. They see opportunities such as eBay as a way to market and focus on their core business, and are not distracted into creating a new business. They know that if they get out there more it will happen. Internet marketers are focused on expanding and building their business, their core business.

Number Five: MARKETING FOCUSED

The fifth characteristic is extremely important. Write it down. These millionaires are focused on marketing. They understand the importance of getting out there and building their email lists so that countless hot hungry people can follow them.

I learned this trait straight from one billionaire that I had the privilege to sit down with. When you meet with a billionaire, you feel his energy. You know these people vibrate on a much higher level, than most of us. It is amazing but when somebody has made that much money, you listen to every word he says to you. You had better listen. Here is what one billionaire said to me that changed my life, *"Matt, if you want to make a decent income, then you sell products and services. But, if you want to become insanely rich, then you create and control markets."* This is being marketing-focused. You go out there and find people who are hot and hungry for what you have to offer. You get in front of them and market your ideas.

My major in college was Marketing. How did I know that Marketing was essential so early on? I didn't... well I didn't understand it at that point. But I had the Microsoft book and studied Bill Gates and he was a Marketing major at Harvard. I said this guy knows something that I don't, that few people do in fact. A few years later, I figured out his secret. I realized that the key to my own business is marketing. Everybody that Bill Gates hires in upper management has a marketing background. Look at how the Microsoft Company has taken over the market share of the whole world. It just goes to show that the Internet Millionaire Mind is Marketing-focused.

Number Six: EDUCATION FOCUSED - UNDERSTAND IMPORTANCE OF CONTINUING EDUCATION

The sixth characteristic shared by Internet Millionaires is understanding the **importance** of continuing education. Internet Millionaires are constantly learning. They learn by attending seminars and reading or listening to home study courses that sharpen their skills in a particular area related to their focus. An important distinction to make is that Millionaires do not listen to just anyone, they seek out experts. Why learn from anyone less than a master?

If you are learning from material created by someone who is only good, not great, then you are learning want they have right and what they have wrong.

For example, right now I am focusing a little on eBay. I found an Internet Millionaire who sold more than $20 million worth of merchandise on eBay from October to May. I was extremely excited, because I only wanted to learn from someone who had become a millionaire selling on eBay. Now, I have been selling our products on eBay as a new avenue, a new route for us to make things happen.

I personally witness this kind of success all the time. It is what I call the Henry Ford effect. Let me tell you a story about Henry Ford and the wisdom that made him one of the two people I admire most. He always surrounded himself with people who were either smarter than he or who had the specialized knowledge that he was looking for. Ford always made sure of that and he invested in these experts that he had carefully selected. You start thinking like Bill Gates and Henry Ford. Read about them. Ask yourself, what would Henry Ford or Bill Gates do. What would they be thinking about?

Number Seven: NOT AFRAID TO MAKE MISTAKES- RECEIVE FEEDBACK

The seventh is also, very important. Highlight it. Internet Millionaires are not afraid of making mistakes. I make mistakes all the time. You have my book. There are mistakes in it. I am correcting the mistakes (but I didn't let it stop me from moving forward either). I sent it to my editor the other day and said, "We've got mistakes. Change it."

The Principle is 'if you stop… you lose.' People fail to get things done, they are perfectionists. You should not always aim for being a perfectionist. It will cause you to stop moving forward. It will cause you to lose your goals. I am learning to let go of perfectionism. Because perfectionism is not always possible. Let go.

You just have to get your message out there. You just get it all going. An old friend Mike Litman says, "You don't have to get right, you just got to get it going."

When you are in Action and you make things happen, you make mistakes. Today, I misspelled psyche. I sent it in an email without catching it. I goofed. In addition, today I am sure that I sent a Matt@ ultraadvance, instead of Matt@powerfulpromoter again. We are all human. We make mistakes. Now here is the goodest thing... oops! Here is the best thing about making mistakes; it is one of the most powerful ways to get feedback.

The world is always giving us feedback. Always. Feedback is a great way to learn. Feedback is a great way to learn because it is honest. This is one of life's gifts to us. People share opinions and give you their points of view, you learn from them. Glean new insight from them and you may change your direction based on what people TELL you they want.

Chapter 4 **Nine Common Characteristics**

Drew Miles, once a client and now a business partner, had been focusing his marketing on asset protection. Then we discovered through feedback, that people were extremely interested in Drew helping them slash their taxes up to 60% to 70%. But were only mildly interested in the asset protection that is part of the same program. We didn't change the business model. We didn't even change the product. We changed our communication to that market. We simply let the same audience hear more about the tax slashing that they are interested in.

Remember feedback is around you all the time. You might have products or services have calls from prospects or even clients that say, "Do you offer _ ___?" or "Aw, man, I wish you would offer this to me." Use the feedback as a starting point; don't take personally or as a failure, take it with a grain of salt. In fact, pat your yourself on the back every time you realize that you just heard a valuable key to offering

your market exactly what they want to buy. Feedback is a great way to learn and grow.

Internet Millionaires are not afraid to make mistakes. They know that mistakes are learning experiences. Remember the first characteristic was about learning, not blaming.

Number Eight: MODEL AND SWIPE

The eight common characteristics of Internet Millionaires is the wisdom to model and swipe. Internet Millionaires model their systems after other people's effective systems. Modeling other systems teaches you successful strategies. When you model, you already know how the system works. For example, somebody sends you an e-mail that influences you to buy. Look the strategies used: the layout, the key words, and the subject line. Look at the things that got you motivated to move forward to take action and to buy from them.

You can learn from that. You want to model successful business owners and you want to model successful Internet Millionaires, but you have to be careful. Make certain that you are modeling a success and not someone that is making a bogus claim.

Be aware that there are **the three types of people: thinkers, talkers, and walkers**.

Thinkers

They are the people who say things like: "Yeah, I thought of that." or "I've been thinking about it."

Talkers

These are the people who always say, "Oh yeah, here's a great idea, this is a great one." Next week, they say, "Oh, here's another great idea, you know here's another great idea. Here is another great idea," and every week and every day there's another great idea, well they're just talkers

Walkers

The people you learn from are the walkers they are making it happen. Model the walkers because they are creating success in their ventures. Success will come

quicker and will be easier that you think. These are the people who are making it happen.

Smart Internet marketers do not argue with success. Internet Millionaire marketers don't argue with the processes and they don't argue with the systems that are already working for someone else. As I love to say, *"You don't go to the bank for originality"*. When I go to the bank to deposit my checks, they don't say, "Was this an original thought?" No, they say thank you and put it in the bank account.

You want what is called a **Swipe File**. Look at what successful marketers are doing that you want to model and store it in a place where you can reference it. I have a folder in my email program for great emails (including ones that I wrote!) and I have a manila folder that holds postcards, letters and print ads that have caught my attention. The other day I was just looking for an innovative idea, I opened my file, and before long, I had my idea.

Realize that there are other marketers in your target market probably sending out emails all the time. Subscribe to somebody's newsletter that is in your niche and keep the emails that really appeal to you. Go buy something from them and learn from it, pay attention to what they do well.

Remember be in Action. Be ready to move, be ready to make things happen. Model successful people, the walkers among us - those who are achieving their goals. Be a walker. Fulfill your dreams.

Number 9: BUILD TEAM "SUCCESS IS A TEAM SPORT"

The ninth common characteristic of an Internet Millionaire is team building. Successful people build teams. I could not have reached my present level of success with utilizing this trait. I have a beautiful wife who supports me emotionally and strategically. I have a great team around me and I have great friends that make things happen. For instance, we support each

other in product launches, by bouncing ideas off each other, and through sharing new ways of market. You must create a great team for your business.

You might ask… "How do you find these people?" I found people like themselves examining my own behavior. Remember, Internet Millionaires are Education Oriented. We are constantly seeking more specialized education. Therefore, I find most of my team at seminars. Stu McLaren and I became accountability partners because we attended the same seminar. I became friends with Armand Morin after seeing him at several seminars.

I have met some of my best friends at seminars. The people are like family because we have something in common. Something that makes us different from our natural families and other friends. Different because not many people are Action Oriented. You took Action when you bought this e-book. You have demonstrated

that you are Education Focused by reading it. We are a little different from most people.

I have also discovered that my best learning experiences come from seminars because I am a visual learner. I am attending an Armand Morin seminar, although I already practice many of the ideas he will present. But I know that he will present at least one new idea that I will use to make more millions.

I am only looking for one nugget at his event. Every meeting and every chat is a learning experience. I know I am going to find five or more joint venture partners. I am going to make many things happen. I am going to find new friends. I will be able to find them. You have to find the players to build your team. Because success, getting rich, is a team sport.

You must have other people around you, supporting you, cheering you on and helping you move forward. The best source is through the seminar. Once, I was a seminar junkie, I went to every seminar I heard about.

Later when my business was taking off. I started going only to marketing seminars. The key to my business is marketing. It doesn't matter what type of business you have. The key to your business is marketing.

When I first met my wife, she was a CFP®, a Certified Financial Planner. She told me she was one of the best financial planners out there. Other people in her company were making more money than she was, even though they were not as skilled as she was at managing people's accounts. They were just better at marketing. It drove her absolutely insane.

Are you in a situation similar to hers? Do you see your competitors attracting more prospects than you do? Do you see people in your industry that might damage their clients because of their character, skill or training, yet they have people flocking to them? The difference between you and them is that they understand that *the key to business is marketing.* You want to build a team around yourself to help you market.

Chapter 5

Powerful Questions Internet Millionaires ASK

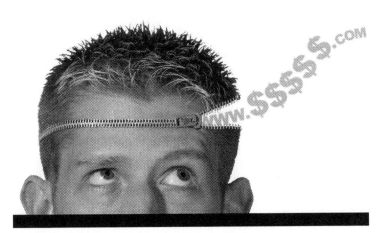

Powerful Questions
Internet Millionaires ASK

Highlight this: Internet Millionaires ask powerful questions. They ask questions beginning with the words what and how. **"What can I do? How can I make my idea happen?"** They do not say why for two reasons. The first is that Why is very negative for many people, myself included. We are reminded of being a child and getting into trouble with the only question being "Why did you do that?" To this day, when somebody says, "Why," I start putting up my guard.

The second reason not to ask why, to yourself, is that you can start too many conversations in your head. The truth is there is rarely an answer to *Why,* so don't get caught up in it. Do not ask why, what you want to do is ask what and ask how. What and how. When you ask questions with **what** and **how**, amazing things happen to you. Those two words can change you and can change outcomes for you on many projects.

In addition to what and how there is a special phrase I use; let me explain the power of **What Right Now**. You might ask yourself this question, if you're stuck in a rut. "Self, I'm flat broke. What is my fastest path to cash? How can I get there? *What* do I need to do *right now*?" When you are bogged down in all the different actions you could take to grow your business ask: What comes first? What should I be doing right now?

Chapter 6

The Two Magic Words Internet Millionaires Use

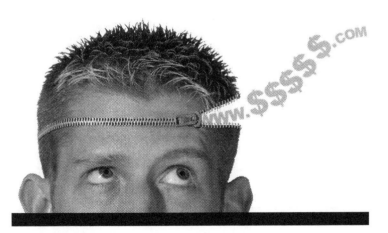

The Two Magic Words Internet Millionaires Use

Internet Millionaires use two magic words (highlight this) when they ask themselves questions or their teams questions. The two words are **Systematize** and **Monetize**. To systematize is to create systems that don't rely on a particular person but instead are run so that any qualified person can be "plugged in" your routine or so that a machine or computer operation can complete the routine. To monetize is to turn your projects into money making ventures. Let me put those two powerful questions with the two magic words.

First, for Systematize you might ask: *How can I systematize my organization?* or *What can I do inside my business to systematize it?* You know that you have a great business, but how can it be systematized? You need to use systems to leverage your results and make bigger things happen. I have thousands of readers subscribing to my lists. Somehow, I have to add them to email list.

You might wonder how you can help systematize this. How can I communicate to my subscribers without having to personally send out each email myself? Your answer could be an autoresponder. This means putting up messages with answers to those questions people are always asking.

Then, for Monetize you might ask: *How can I monetize my efforts?* or *What can I do inside my business to monetize it?* You know that you have a great idea, but how can it be monetized? If you can't monetize it, most times, you must say okay, let's scratch this idea and move to the next one.

Chapter 7
Action Steps

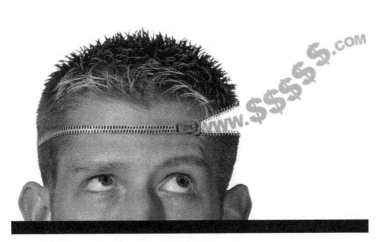

Action Steps

There's one thing that is not shared much at all. And I'm talking about something that affects you when you are getting started. You have to make **Sacrifices**. I made sacrifices. Sacrifices are a given in the early period of your business. In fact, I want to share with you a story that most people don't realize. It's a story from the book Walking with the Wise by *Mentors Magazine* that I'm also featured in. This piece is by Donald Trump that I want to share with you. In his article, Trump lists the top 10 ways of thinking like a billionaire, a billionaire not millionaire. I want share 3 of them with you.

1) **Don't take vacations.** This is Trump's way #1 and it is a sacrifice. It does help to be passionate about your business. And this is completely necessary unless you want to lose your momentum when you are getting started.

2) Have a short-term attention span. Personally, I have ADHD so that has always been true for me.

3) Don't sleep any more than you have to. You have probably not been told that before, but Trump says one of the top 10 ways to think like a billionaire is don't sleep any more than you have to.

Trump wrote, "I usually sleep about four hours per night. I'm in bed by 1 am and up to read the newspaper by 5 am. That's all I need, and it gives me a competitive edge. I have friends who are successful and sleep ten hours a night, and I ask them, 'How can you compete against people like me if I sleep only four hours?'" (Did you notice the powerful question: "How can you compete against people like me?") He goes on to say that no matter how brilliant you are there are not enough hours in a day. The point is success can rarely be accomplished with 10 hours sleep which equals a day that is only 14 hours long.

Chapter 7 **Action Steps**

I can tell you that many times I have **sacrificed** my sleep. Sometimes I have sacrificed my credit rating and even my financial security. I could make the sacrifices because they were a product of my decisive action. I had made a decision that I was going to do whatever it took to get in a position of financial independence - where I am at right now - because I knew that would allow me to be able to relax and enjoy and to do all these things. And to not have any worries. Even though I am 28, I could retire now right now if I chose to. Retire for the rest of my life with the investments we have and from the money that we make off our businesses.

In addition, it is absolutely powerful, this mindset that I'm sharing with you. But when I made the decision, I began to make some sacrifices. When I first got into the information world, I got my start working behind the scenes with the Robert Kiyosaki organization. I would get phone calls to my Georgia residence, three days before they were meeting and they would say, "Matt, we need you to come to

Phoenix." "We need you to come to San Francisco." We need you here or there and I did whatever it took to make that appointment.

I did it because I knew there would be contacts that I could learn from. These were people who were making things happen. Then there were the "Oh yeah, Matt, you need you to go to this seminar." I didn't have the money. I don't even know how I did it.

I had faith and I knew things would happen. With no notice, I would fly across the country. I would go to the seminars where I met amazing people who changed my life. They instilled in me nuggets of wisdom that allowed me to get to the place I am now.

Maybe you are experiencing some feelings of uncertainty or FEAR. I can honestly tell you that I do not regret any of these sacrifices. You have to make sacrifices. Maybe right now you have a little bit of hesitation, but just imagine how it is going to be for you when things change. All of a sudden, WOW!, you can make that money that you've always wanted.

Here are some Action Steps called the **Internet Millionaire Actions Steps**. I remember a couple of friends and I were like kids dreaming about the business and life that I have right now. Dreams become reality, if you have faith and work hard. I used to do what I called the Cell Phone Challenge. I still use this technique, but today I am more aggressive.

Here are your Action Steps for the **Cell Phone Challenge**. Pull out your cell phone right now. Look at every contact in your cell phone directory or your rolodex. Consider those people, saved in your cell phone, that are taking your energy, who are dragging you down, and who are telling you that you cannot accomplish your goals. The next step is extremely important - *delete their names* from your cell phone. Eliminate obstacles in your path to success. This

might prove somewhat difficult, I know it hurt me the first time.

When every call I receive from a person leaves me bombarded by griping and complaining, moaning and groaning; I know I have to do the Cell Phone Challenge. When you get rid of the people that pull you down, you open up a space on your cell phone for somebody who is at a higher level. Somebody who's going to come to you, somebody you can learn from. Within a short time, the space would be filled with someone who became a great friend, mentor or contact. Remember eliminate contacts and acquaintances who bring you down, I challenge you to do the Cell Phone Challenge right now!

Beyond the Cell Phone Challenge, I used to enter in my contact list the names of people that I wanted to meet. Many times when I put a name in, I was amazed to meet the person at a seminar or business meeting. Things fall into place. The contact would give me his phone number and suddenly I had a new best friend. This is a powerful step.

Next Action Step: **Stop that negative mind chatter**. Have you ever heard these gremlins inside your head that are talking to you all the time? You know all that negative self-talk? You have to stop that and you want to replace it by telling yourself positive things. Start using decisive language such as "I will do this, I must do this. I can make it. I will reach my goals." Never say to yourself that you can't.

You probably hear a relentless mom or another voice nagging you. My critical voice made interaction with others difficult at times. It was an obstacle to peaceful. Stop that negative mind chatter; finally, I stopped the chatter.

Replace the negatism things you need for them to be. When I did, after that I was like, "Oh, my gosh." I started becoming who I wanted to become. I started taking action. It strengthened my faith. Amazing

things started happening to me. You want to stop those gremlins.

Remember I said that I was going to share a secret that I have never shared in public. Well, I had to have faith to share this. I told you earlier that a couple of friends and I used to dream together. We also began our million-dollar run together. We had these private conversations because we were that success team that I was telling you that you must have. We would build each other up.

We also developed some of our current Millionaire Mindset. And here's one of the things we used to tell each other. You know what we used to say to those gremlins in our head? We took on the FU attitude. You to have to have the FU attitude. You can say it anyway, you want. That's the way I could stop the negative chatter. I would say, I'm going to go forward. I'm going to make this happen. I won't let anything stop me.

And you've got to take that on that mindset and make it happen for yourself. You have to stop all those negative things that are around you and start moving forward so you can move into action so you can get the results that you want. If you don't, you're going stay right where you are now. You have to. You absolutely must go out there and make that happen.

Here's another Action Step for you: The secret to success is becoming a master marketer. **You <u>must</u> become a master marketer**. Do you know the difference between marketing and sales? In my opinion, *sales* is one to one. While **marketing is one to many**. Through marketing, you are able to change many lives. Marketing is huge. Bill Gates knew it. Henry Ford knew it. Morgan knew it. Armand knows it. These successful men all knew that marketing is the key to your success. I know it and now you know it. You must become a master marketer.

> **Internet Millionaire Mindset**
> ### Action Steps
> ✂ Cell Phone Challenge
>
> ✂ Stop the Negative Mind Chatter
>
> ✂ Challenge -Actively Start Seeking
>   Marketing Education
>
> ✂ Become A Master Marketer
>
> ✂ It's Your Right and Your Responsibility
>
> PowerfulPromoter.com

You must actively go there in your mindset and your actions. I challenge you, to start seeking marketing education, because marketing is the most important element of your business. You have products. You have services. Even if you just have an idea, it is your right to go out there. It's your responsibility to be out there learning how to get your ideas, your products, and your services out to the public. Because if you don't, you're not only ripping me off, you're not only ripping everybody in your local area 1 off, but you're also ripping the world off. And you know what? You're not only ripping all of us off, you're also ripping yourself off, because you could be putting a lot of money in your back pocket that you're not. Just imagine how it would be for you if you had an extra $10,000. Just imagine how it would be with an extra $100,000, maybe even another $1 million.

You can make that happen, because it's your right, your responsibility. You must get out there and market, persuade and make people aware of what you have to offer.

A while back, I was talking to a man who sells security alarms. I sensed that he had a problem and asked what was wrong. He told me that a few weeks earlier he had gotten a call from clients who wanted their house checked and an alarm installed. He felt lazy that day. He decided not to accept the responsibility. He let it slide. He sat on his butt and watched TV instead.

Well, he had just found out that on the day after he skipped out on the install, the couple had gotten broken into and their family's things were stolen. And worse yet, they did bad things to the family.

That's similar to what I'm talking about right here. It's your right and it's your responsibility to go out there and market to people. I don't care what you're selling. I don't care what you have. I don't care what your ideas are. You must find people who know how to systemize things. You must find people who know how to monetize things. When you do your dreams and plans will start coming true. You'll learn how to market your business. You'll learn how to make money. It's your job. It's your right, it's your responsibility.

By now, you've learned that it's your right, and it's your responsibility to go out there and make that happen. We've talked about the Nine Common Characteristics of Internet Millionaires. Remember what those are. What's the difference between a business models — there's a bankruptcy model and there's Millionaire model? Remember that's about focus. We talked about Internet Millionaire accidents. We talked about the statistics of Internet millionaires or millionaires out there right now.

There are so many things for you to do. It's your job, and it's your right to get your information out there. I want to tell you that it's been an honor and it's been a privilege to write this book for you. I want to tell you I appreciate you. And it's awesome, because we're no different. I'm just like you. I care; I've been in your shoes. This Mindset will change your life.